MAJOR BATTLES IN US HISTORY

THE TET OFFENSIVE

CRUCIAL BATTLES OF THE VIETNAM WAR

by Katy Duffield

WWW.NORTHSTAREDITIONS.COM

Produced for North Star Editions by Red Line Editorial.

Photographs ©: Dang Van Phuoc/AP Images, cover, 1; Red Line Editorial, 5; AP Images, 6–7, 9, 11, 16, 24–25; Bettmann/Getty Images, 12–13; Vietnam News Agency/AP Images, 18–19; Horst Faas/AP Images, 21; Dan Simonsen/Shutterstock Images, 22; Everett Collection/Newscom, 27

Content Consultant: James H. Willbanks, PhD, General of the Army George C. Marshall Chair of Military History, US Army Command and General Staff College

ISBN
978-1-63517-025-2 (hardcover)
978-1-63517-081-8 (paperback)
978-1-63517-185-3 (ebook pdf)
978-1-63517-135-8 (hosted ebook)

Library of Congress Control Number: 2016951029

Printed in the United States of America
Mankato, MN
November, 2016

ABOUT THE AUTHOR

Katy Duffield has a bachelor's degree in English from the University of Illinois-Springfield. She is the author of more than 20 books for children and has written both fiction and nonfiction for many children's magazines.

TABLE OF CONTENTS

1954: Vietnam is split in two. North Vietnam officially becomes a Communist country.

1959: Communists from North Vietnam begin traveling to South Vietnam to rebel against the South Vietnamese government.

1962: The United States increases the number of military advisers in South Vietnam.

1965: US combat troops arrive in South Vietnam.

1968: Starting on January 30, Communists launch the Tet Offensive against the South Vietnamese government. In March, the main phase of the offensive is defeated.

1969: The United States begins to pull out its troops from Vietnam.

1973: A cease-fire agreement is established in Vietnam. All US troops pull out.

1975: The North Vietnamese launch new attacks and take control of South Vietnam.

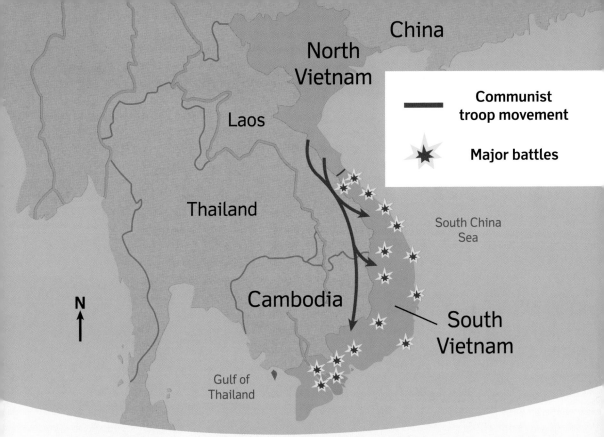

TET OFFENSIVE: ESTIMATED DEATHS

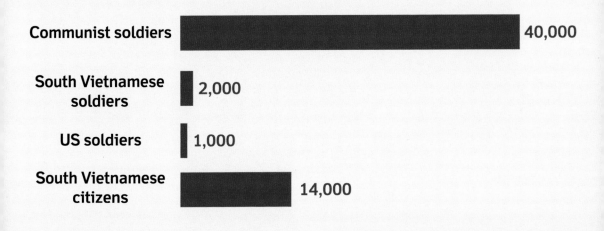

Communist soldiers	40,000
South Vietnamese soldiers	2,000
US soldiers	1,000
South Vietnamese citizens	14,000

CHAPTER 1

US EMBASSY ATTACKED!

In the early hours of January 31, 1968, 19 men put on black clothing and red armbands. They readied their weapons. They had AK-47 rifles, rocket-propelled grenades, and C-4 explosives. Some of the men climbed into a truck. Others got into a taxicab. They drove through Saigon, the capital of South Vietnam.

Rebel fighters stand at attention in a jungle in South Vietnam.

The men were members of the Vietnamese **Communist** movement, or Vietcong. Soon, they saw their target: the US **embassy**. The Vietcong placed explosives next to the 8-foot (2.4-m) concrete wall that surrounded the embassy buildings. A loud explosion ripped a 3-foot (0.9-m) hole in the wall.

Vietcong invaders scrambled into the embassy **compound**. Two US military police (MPs) raced to the area with guns drawn. Shots rang out. Two Vietcong fell. One of the MPs radioed for help. Then a hail of bullets from the Vietcong brought down both MPs. Two US Marines inside the embassy heard the commotion

Two military police officers help a wounded MP during the attack on the US embassy in Saigon.

and jumped into action. One grabbed a telephone to report the attack to another officer inside the embassy. The other locked the heavy wooden doors that led into the embassy's main building.

At that moment, a rocket exploded against the doors. The guard on the phone was thrown to the floor. He suffered a broken leg and a serious head injury.

Reports of the attack spread quickly around Saigon. US soldiers rushed to help. The Vietnam War (1955–1975) had been going on for multiple years, and many US troops were stationed around the city. A US helicopter tried to land on the embassy's roof. But heavy enemy gunfire forced it to turn back. Later, other helicopters were able to land at the embassy. Armed US soldiers hopped onto the roof. They searched the main

Military police lead a captured Vietcong fighter from the US embassy on January 31, 1968.

embassy building. No Vietcong were in the building. But some were still inside the compound. The US and Vietcong soldiers continued to fight. More than six hours after the battle began, the US embassy was finally secured. All Vietcong attackers were killed or captured.

CHAPTER 2

A DIVIDED VIETNAM

The attack on Saigon was part of a much bigger campaign called the Tet Offensive. The army of North Vietnam, together with the Vietcong, had been fighting against the army of South Vietnam since the mid-1950s. The North Vietnamese force consisted of a traditional army invading from the north.

North Vietnamese military leader Vo Nguyen Giap (front) examines a row of soldiers.

The Vietcong were **guerrillas** who lived in South Vietnam and supported the North Vietnamese army's cause. Some Vietcong guerillas did not wear uniforms. Because they looked like regular **civilians**, the fighters were difficult to identify.

The governments of North and South Vietnam had very different beliefs. Leaders of the North wanted Vietnam to be a single Communist country. The leaders of South Vietnam did not want their country to be Communist. US leaders wanted to stop the spread of Communism throughout the world. So the United States joined South Vietnam in its fight against the North. By 1967,

US combat troops had been fighting alongside the South Vietnamese forces for approximately two years. North Vietnamese leaders were creating plans they hoped would end the war.

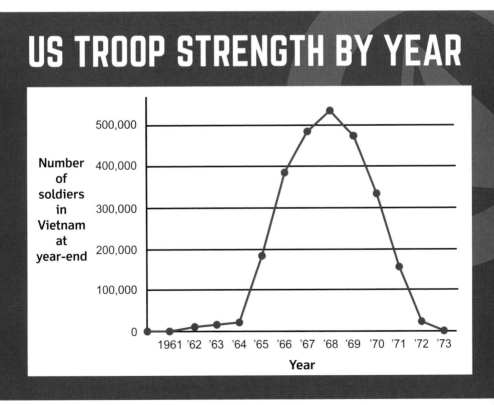

US TROOP STRENGTH BY YEAR

Number of soldiers in Vietnam at year-end

Year

Vietcong guerrillas established bases in remote areas of South Vietnam.

North Vietnamese politicians Le Duan and Le Duc Tho called for a series of surprise attacks against areas that had not yet been attacked. The plan called for a huge buildup of troops and weapons. Approximately 80,000 Vietcong and

North Vietnamese secretly moved into their positions within South Vietnam.

US officials noticed the increased activity in South Vietnam. At first, they thought people were preparing for a New Year's celebration called Tet. But US general William Westmoreland thought the increased movement might mean a big attack was coming. However, he was not sure when or where it might occur.

In past years, the North and South had agreed to stop fighting during Tet. But in 1968, the North Vietnamese decided to ignore the **cease-fire**. They hoped an attack during Tet would catch US and South Vietnamese troops off guard.

CHAPTER 3

SURPRISE ATTACKS

The first attack of the Tet Offensive was a distraction. On January 21, 1968, North Vietnamese soldiers began shelling a US base in Khe Sanh, South Vietnam. The US military focused on protecting the base. Then, on January 30, the Vietcong attacked 13 South Vietnamese cities. But that was only the beginning.

Soldiers carry a North Vietnamese flag into battle.

On the morning of January 31, more than 100 cities were attacked.

In Saigon, North Vietnamese troops and Vietcong guerillas flooded the streets. They targeted air bases, government buildings, and military posts. The Communists bombarded their targets with rocket and **mortar** blasts. They launched ground assaults with grenades, assault rifles, and light machine guns.

As the battle raged in Saigon, the Vietcong attacked other areas in the South. In Da Nang, the South Vietnamese army fought to protect its headquarters. And by 5:00 a.m., important army bases in Long Binh and Bien Hoa were

US soldiers land in an open field on their way to join South Vietnamese troops fighting the Vietcong.

also under direct Vietcong attack. Across South Vietnam, US and South Vietnamese soldiers found themelves under attack.

US and South Vietnamese troops were not ready for the surprise attacks. But the militaries quickly made adjustments.

Additional US and South Vietnamese troops rushed to help. US troops forced the attackers back with large mounted guns called howitzers. Fighter planes bombed the enemy from the air.

THE SPOOKY GUNSHIP

Soldiers aboard the Spooky, an AC-47 gunship, were able to stop or slow enemy attacks and help reduce damage and losses on the ground.

Firepower: Three side-mounted miniguns capable of firing hundreds of rounds per minute

Wingspan: 95 feet (29 m)

Top Speed: 220 mph (354 km/h)

Helicopters transported troops and provided cover for soldiers on the ground.

Intense firefights rocked South Vietnam. But in most areas, the Communist forces were pushed back quickly. The Vietcong did not have the firepower to compete with the US and South Vietnamese troops. The Vietcong were unable to control any of the places they attacked.

Some battles lasted longer, however. Fighting in Saigon lasted several days. The battle in the city of Hue raged for more than three weeks. By the end of February 1968, the main phase of the Tet Offensive had ended.

CHAPTER 4

AFTERMATH OF THE OFFENSIVE

The Tet Offensive was a costly campaign. Thousands of soldiers on both sides lost their lives. Buildings were reduced to heaps of rubble. Innocent civilians suffered terrible injuries, and thousands were killed. Other civilians found themselves without homes.

US Marines rest along a broken wall in Hue. Fighting in Hue was among the bloodiest in the war.

The North Vietnamese did not achieve the victory they had hoped for. But their plan was successful in some ways. The attacks shocked and surprised US and South Vietnamese troops. Northern leaders believed the offensive took away any hope the United States had of winning the war.

General Westmoreland believed his troops had triumphed on the battlefield. They had stopped the Vietcong from taking over South Vietnam. Many of the attackers had been killed. But many Americans felt differently. Americans had watched television coverage of the offensive. They did not want to spend

US television reporters conduct an interview with a
US Army officer in Hue, South Vietnam.

more money or lose any more soldiers in
the Vietnam War.

President Lyndon B. Johnson thought
about sending more US troops to
Vietnam. In the end, he agreed to send
a small number of additional troops.
However, he did not send the 206,000
soldiers requested by Westmoreland.

Johnson also considered more bombing raids against the North. But huge **protests** against the war made him reconsider.

The Tet Offensive was a turning point in the Vietnam War. The US and South Vietnamese fighters won the battle.

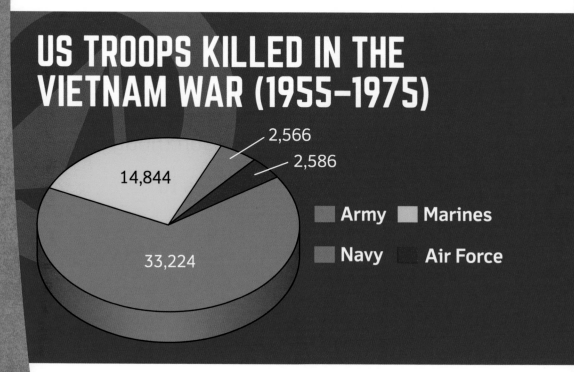

US TROOPS KILLED IN THE VIETNAM WAR (1955–1975)

2,566
2,586
14,844
33,224

Army   Marines

Navy   Air Force

But the offensive made many Americans think they would not win the war.

On March 31, 1968, Johnson gave a speech. He said he would stop bombing North Vietnam if its leaders would talk about ending the war. Also, because many people disapproved of his handling of the war, he announced he would not run for reelection. Fighting in Vietnam continued over the next several years, but peace talks began as well. US troops slowly withdrew. After they left, the South Vietnamese were unable to hold off the North Vietnamese. In the spring of 1975, North Vietnamese forces captured Saigon and took control of the South.

FOCUS ON
THE TET OFFENSIVE

Write your answers on a separate piece of paper.

1. Summarize the reasons for the United States entering and exiting the Vietnam War.

2. Why do you think seeing video footage of the war changed Americans' views of the war?

3. Which of these fought against the spread of Communism?

      A. Vietcong

      B. North Vietnamese

      C. South Vietnamese

4. Which of the following may have occurred had protests over the war not broken out in the United States?

      A. The United States may have sent many more troops to South Vietnam.

      B. The United States may have pulled out of the war sooner.

      C. Peace talks between the North and South Vietnamese may have started sooner.

Answer key on page 32.

GLOSSARY

cease-fire
An agreement to stop fighting for a period of time.

civilians
People who are not in the military.

Communist
Having to do with a political system in which all property is owned by the government.

compound
A collection of buildings enclosed by a wall or fence.

embassy
A building where representatives from another country live or work.

guerrillas
Fighters who use surprise attacks and are not part of a regular army.

mortar
A lightweight cannon that shoots shells high in the air.

protests
Public expressions of disapproval or disagreement.

TO LEARN MORE

BOOKS

Dunn, Joeming W. *Tet Offensive.* Minneapolis: Abdo, 2016.

Englar, Mary. *The Tet Offensive.* Minneapolis: Compass Point, 2009.

Samuels, Charlie. *The Tet Offensive.* New York: Gareth Stevens, 2014.

NOTES TO EDUCATORS

Visit **www.focusreaders.com** to find lesson plans, activities, links, and other resources related to this title.

INDEX

Answer Key: 1. Answers will vary; **2.** Answers will vary; **3.** C; **4.** A